LIVING
the WISDOM
of the TAO

THE COMPLETE TAO TE CHING
AND AFFIRMATIONS

Also by Dr. Wayne W. Dyer

<u>BOOKS</u>

Being in Balance

Change Your Thoughts—Change Your Life

Everyday Wisdom

Everyday Wisdom for Success

Getting in the Gap (book-with-CD)

Gifts from Eykis

Incredible You! (children's book with Kristina Tracy)

Inspiration

The Invisible Force

It's Not What You've Got! (children's book with Kristina Tracy)

Manifest Your Destiny

A Morning and Afternoon of Your Life

A New Way of Thinking, a New Way of Being
(available August 2009)

No More Holiday Blues

The Power of Intention

A Promise Is a Promise

Pulling Your Own Strings

Real Magic

The Sky's the Limit

Staying on the Path

10 Secrets for Success and Inner Peace

There Is a Spiritual Solution to Every Problem

Unstoppable Me! (children's book with Kristina Tracy)

What Do You Really Want for Your Children?

Wisdom of the Ages

You'll See It When You Believe It

Your Erroneous Zones

Your Sacred Self

Your Ultimate Calling

AUDIO/CD PROGRAMS

Applying the 10 Secrets for Success and Inner Peace
Change Your Thoughts—Change Your Life
(unabridged audio book)
Change Your Thoughts Meditation
Everyday Wisdom (audio book)
Freedom Through Higher Awareness
How to Be a No-Limit Person
How to Get What You Really, Really, Really, Really Want
If You Change the Way You Live, the Life You Are Living Will Change (abridged 4-CD set)
Inspiration (abridged 4-CD set)
Inspirational Thoughts
The Keys to Higher Awareness
Making Your Thoughts Work for You (with Byron Katie)
Meditations for Manifesting
A Morning and Afternoon of Your Life (abridged 4-CD set)
101 Ways to Transform Your Life (audio book)
The Power of Intention (abridged 4-CD set)
A Promise Is a Promise (audio book)
The Secrets of the Power of Intention (6-CD set)
10 Secrets for Success and Inner Peace
There Is a Spiritual Solution to Every Problem
The Wayne Dyer Audio Collection/CD Collection
Your Journey to Enlightenment (6-tape program)

VIDEOCASSETTES

Creating Real Magic in Your Life
How to Be a No-Limit Person
The Miracle Mindset
10 Secrets for Success and Inner Peace
What Do You Really Want for Your Children?

MISCELLANEOUS

Change Your Thoughts—Change Your Life Perpetual Flip Calendar
(available August 2008)
Everyday Wisdom Perpetual Flip Calendar
Inner Peace Cards
Inspiration Cards
Inspiration Perpetual Flip Calendar
The Power of Intention Cards
The Power of Intention Perpetual Flip Calendar
10 Secrets for Success and Inner Peace Cards
10 Secrets for Success and Inner Peace gift products:
<u>*Notecards, Candle,*</u> and <u>*Journal*</u>

All of the above are available at your local bookstore,
or may be ordered by visiting:

Hay House USA: **www.hayhouse.com**®
Hay House Australia: **www.hayhouse.com.au**
Hay House UK: **www.hayhouse.co.uk**
Hay House South Africa: **www.hayhouse.co.za**
Hay House India: **www.hayhouse.co.in**

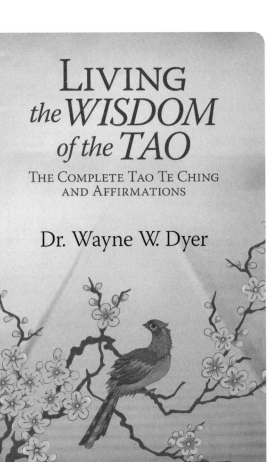

LIVING
the WISDOM
of the TAO

THE COMPLETE TAO TE CHING
AND AFFIRMATIONS

Dr. Wayne W. Dyer

HAY HOUSE, INC.
Carlsbad, California • New York City
London • Sydney • Johannesburg
Vancouver • Hong Kong • New Delhi

Published and distributed in the United States by: Hay House, Inc.: www.
hayhouse.com • **Published and distributed in Australia by:** Hay House
Australia Pty. Ltd.: www.hayhouse.com.au • **Published and distributed in the
United Kingdom by:** Hay House UK, Ltd.: www.hayhouse.co.uk • **Published and
distributed in the Republic of South Africa by:** Hay House SA (Pty), Ltd.: www.
hayhouse.co.za • **Distributed in Canada by:** Raincoast: www.raincoast.com
• **Published in India by:** Hay House Publishers India: www.hayhouse.co.in

Editorial supervision: Jill Kramer • *Design:* Amy Rose Grigoriou

Library of Congress Cataloging-in-Publication Data

Dyer, Wayne W.
  Living the Wisdom of the Tao: The complete tao te ching and affirmations /
Wayne W. Dyer.
      p. cm.
  ISBN-13: 978-1-4019-2149-1 (tradepaper) 1. Laozi. Dao de jing. 2. Adaptation,
Psychological. 3. Lifestyle. 4. Thinking. I. Title.
  BL1900.L35D94 2008
  299.5'1482--dc22

                                    2007038306

ISBN: 978-1-4019-2149-1

11 10 09 08   5 4 3 2
1st edition, March 2008
2nd edition, March 2008

Printed in the United States of America

For Kerry.
10,000 thank you's
for your beautiful soul.

Introduction

This book offers you an opportunity to internalize and directly experience the great wisdom of the Tao Te Ching, a collection of 81 verses authored by Lao-tzu, a Chinese prophet who was also the keeper of the imperial archives in the ancient capital of Luoyang. Seeing the continual decay during a period of warring states, Lao-tzu decided to ride westward into the desert. At the Hanku Pass, a gatekeeper named Yin Hsi, knowing of Lao-tzu's reputation for being a man of wisdom, begged him to record the essence of his teaching. Thus, the Tao Te Ching was born out of 5,000 Chinese characters some 25 centuries ago.

The words *Tao Te Ching* translate to "living and applying the Great Way." The Tao is considered by many scholars to be the wisest book ever written. Although it is just 81 short verses, it encourages you to change your life by literally changing the way you think. By reading through the verses presented here (which I've pieced together after reviewing hundreds of translations*)—along with the corresponding affirmation I've created for each verse—you'll be embarking on a path that encompasses the profound ideas that Lao-tzu intended to convey.

By absorbing these powerful new thoughts and imprinting them onto your consciousness, you will begin to see the world and all of its people in a new way. That is precisely what it has done for me. Reading the Tao and incorporating this philosophy into my life has changed me forever.

I created this book to provide you with a simple yet direct experience for changing your thoughts and ultimately changing your life. Through the steady use of this relaxing Tao-centered work, you will begin to live in harmony with your own nature, feeling more at home than you ever felt before and living what is called a truly God-realized life.

The Tao Te Ching offers you Divine guidance on virtually every area of human existence. It is a new way of thinking in a world that needs to recapture its ancient teachings. Work with the verses and affirmations regularly and you will come to know the truth behind the ancient Tao observation: *When you change the way you look at things, the things you look at change.*

I send you much love.

— **Dr. Wayne W. Dyer**

*Author's Note

Some versions of the Tao I relied upon more than others, and I would like to especially mention that the version provided by Jonathan Star (in *Tao Te Ching: the Definitive Edition*) was the one I quoted most extensively and the one that most resonated with my vision and interpretation of the Tao. (In particular, major portions of verses 6, 13, 18, 29, 30, 33, 38, 39, 44, 46, 49, 54, 56, 58, 62, 67, 69, 72, 74, 76, and 79 were quoted from Star's translation.)

I would recommend that anyone seeking to gain a greater insight into the verses of the Tao Te Ching—something that could deepen one's understanding of the ideas provided in this book—should consult Jonathan Star's version. His edition of the Tao Te Ching is unique in that it not only provides an elegant translation of the verses, but also provides a word-for-word translation of every Chinese character found in the original text. By use of this verbatim translation, even those who do not know ancient Chinese can gain a significant insight into the meaning of the original work.

I choose to

enjoy living

the great mystery.

The Tao that can be

named is not the Tao.

1st Verse

The Tao that can be told
is not the eternal Tao.
The name that can be named
is not the eternal name.

The Tao is both named and nameless.
As nameless it is the origin of all things;
as named it is the Mother of 10,000 things.

Ever desireless, one can see the mystery;
ever desiring, one sees only the manifestations.
And the mystery itself is the doorway to
all understanding.

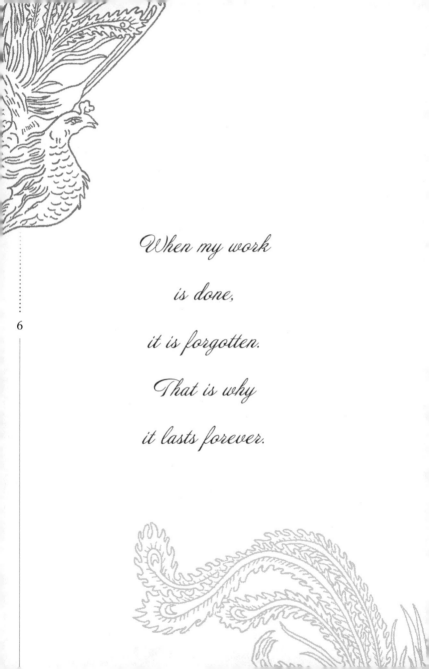

When my work

is done,

it is forgotten.

That is why

it lasts forever.

2nd Verse

Under heaven all can see beauty as beauty,
only because there is ugliness.
All can know good as good only because there is evil.

Being and nonbeing produce each other.
The difficult is born in the easy.
Long is defined by short, the high by the low.
Before and after go along with each other.

So the sage lives openly with apparent duality
and paradoxical unity.
The sage can act without effort
and teach without words.
Nurturing things without possessing them,
he works, but not for rewards;
he competes, but not for results.

When the work is done, it is forgotten.
That is why it lasts forever.

I know that there

is no <u>way</u> to happiness.

Happiness is the <u>Way</u>.

3rd Verse

Putting a value on status
will create contentiousness.
If you overvalue possessions,
people begin to steal.
By not displaying what is desirable, you will
cause the people's hearts to remain undisturbed.

The sage governs
by emptying minds and hearts,
by weakening ambitions and strengthening bones.

Practice not doing. . . .
When action is pure and selfless,
everything settles into its own perfect place.

The all-providing

Tao is empty,

yet inexhaustible.

4th Verse

The Tao is empty
but inexhaustible,
bottomless,
the ancestor of it all.

Within it, the sharp edges become smooth;
the twisted knots loosen;
the sun is softened by a cloud;
the dust settles into place.

It is hidden but always present.
I do not know who gave birth to it.
It seems to be the common ancestor of all,
the father of things.

I work at

eliminating all

of my judgments

of others.

5th Verse

Heaven and earth are impartial;
they see the 10,000 things as straw dogs.
The sage is not sentimental;
he treats all his people as straw dogs.

The sage is like heaven and earth:
To him none are especially dear,
nor is there anyone he disfavors.
He gives and gives, without condition,
offering his treasures to everyone.

Between heaven and earth
is a space like a bellows;
empty and inexhaustible,
the more it is used, the more it produces.

Hold on to the center.
Man was made to sit quietly and find
the truth within.

14

I pay attention

to my inner callings

and apply my

own uniqueness

to everything

I undertake.

6th Verse

The spirit that never dies
is called the mysterious feminine.
Although she becomes the whole universe,
her immaculate purity is never lost.
Although she assumes countless forms,
her true identity remains intact.

The gateway to the mysterious female
is called the root of creation.

Listen to her voice,
hear it echo through creation.
Without fail, she reveals her presence.
Without fail, she brings us to our own perfection.
Although it is invisible, it endures;
it will never end.

It is through selfless

action that I experience

my own fulfillment.

7th Verse

Heaven is eternal—the earth endures.
Why do heaven and earth last forever?
They do not live for themselves only.
This is the secret of their durability.

For this reason the sage puts himself last
and so ends up ahead.
He stays a witness to life,
so he endures.

Serve the needs of others,
and all your own needs will be fulfilled.
Through selfless action, fulfillment is attained.

I live in accordance

with nature and therefore

never go against

the way of things.

8th Verse

The supreme good is like water,
which nourishes all things without trying to.
It flows to low places loathed by all men.
Therefore, it is like the Tao.

Live in accordance with the nature of things.
In dwelling, be close to the land.
In meditation, go deep in the heart.
In dealing with others, be gentle and kind.
Stand by your word.
Govern with equity.
Be timely in choosing the right moment.

One who lives in accordance with nature
does not go against the way of things.
He moves in harmony with the present moment,
always knowing the truth of just what to do.

20

When my cup is full,

I stop pouring.

9th Verse

*To keep on filling
is not as good as stopping.
Overfilled, the cupped hands drip,
better to stop pouring.*

*Sharpen a blade too much
and its edge will soon be lost.
Fill your house with jade and gold
and it brings insecurity.
Puff yourself with honor and pride
and no one can save you from a fall.*

*Retire when the work is done;
this is the way of heaven.*

I suspend

my belief in opposites

by seeing myself in all.

10th Verse

Carrying body and soul
and embracing the one,
can you avoid separation?

Can you let your body become
as supple as a newborn child's?
In the opening and shutting of heaven's gate,
can you play the feminine part?

Can you love your people
and govern your domain
without self-importance?

Giving birth and nourishing;
having, yet not possessing;
working, yet not taking credit;
leading without controlling or dominating.

One who heeds this power
brings the Tao to this very earth.
This is the primal virtue.

The usefulness

of what is depends

on what is not.

11th Verse

Thirty spokes converge upon a single hub;
it is on the hole in the center that
the use of the cart hinges.

Shape clay into a vessel;
it is the space within that makes it useful.
Carve fine doors and windows,
but the room is useful in its emptiness.

The usefulness of what is
depends on what is not.

I choose to ignore

the seductive lure of

acquisition and fame.

12th Verse

The five colors blind the eye.
The five tones deafen the ear.
The five flavors dull the taste.
The chase and the hunt craze people's minds.

Wasting energy to obtain rare objects
only impedes one's growth.

The master observes the world
but trusts his inner vision.
He allows things to come and go.
He prefers what is within to what is without.

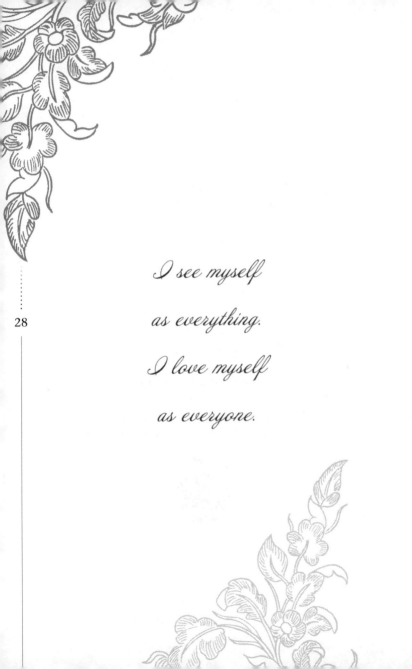

I see myself

as everything.

I love myself

as everyone.

13th Verse

Favor and disgrace seem alarming.
High status greatly afflicts your person.

Why are favor and disgrace alarming?
Seeking favor is degrading:
alarming when it is gotten,
alarming when it is lost.

Why does high status greatly afflict your person?
The reason we have a lot of trouble
is that we have selves.
If we had no selves,
what trouble would we have?

Man's true self is eternal,
yet he thinks, <u>I am this body and will soon die.</u>
If we have no body, what calamities can we have?
One who sees himself as everything
is fit to be guardian of the world.
One who loves himself as everyone
is fit to be teacher of the world.

Discovering how things

have always been brings

me into harmony

with the Way.

14th Verse

That which cannot be seen is called invisible.
That which cannot be heard is called inaudible.
That which cannot be held is called intangible.
These three cannot be defined;
therefore, they are merged as one.

Each of these three is subtle for description.
By intuition you can see it,
hear it,
and feel it.
Then the unseen,
unheard,
and untouched
are present as one.

Its rising brings no dawn,
its setting no darkness;
it goes on and on, unnameable,
returning into nothingness.

Approach it and there is no beginning;
follow it and there is no end.
You cannot know it, but you can be it,
at ease in your own life.

Discovering how things have always been
brings one into harmony with the Way.

The place

of my origination

is stillness, from which

all creation originates.

15th Verse

The ancient masters were profound and subtle.
Their wisdom was unfathomable.
There is no way to describe it.
One can only describe them vaguely
by their appearance.

Watchful, like men crossing a winter stream.
Alert, like men aware of danger.
Simple as uncarved wood.
Hollow like caves.
Yielding, like ice about to melt.
Amorphous, like muddy water.

But the muddiest water clears
as it is stilled.
And out of that stillness
life arises.

He who keeps the Tao does not want to be full.
But precisely because he is never full,
he can remain like a hidden sprout
and does not rush to early ripening.

Amidst the rush

of worldly comings and goings,

I observe how all

endings become beginnings.

16th Verse

Become totally empty.
Let your heart be at peace.
Amidst the rush of worldly comings and goings,
observe how endings become beginnings.

Things flourish, each by each,
only to return to the Source . . .
to what is and what is to be.

To return to the root is to find peace.
To find peace is to fulfill one's destiny.
To fulfill one's destiny is to be constant.
To know the constant is called insight.
Not knowing this cycle
leads to eternal disaster.

Knowing the constant gives perspective.
This perspective is impartial.
Impartiality is the highest nobility;
the highest nobility is Divine.

Being Divine, you will be at one with the Tao.
Being at one with the Tao is eternal.
This way is everlasting,
not endangered by physical death.

I fully trust

that others do know

what is best for them.

17th Verse

With the greatest leader above them,
people barely know one exists.
Next comes one whom they love and praise.
Next comes one whom they fear.
Next comes one whom they despise and defy.

When a leader trusts no one,
no one trusts him.

The great leader speaks little.
He never speaks carelessly.
He works without self-interest
and leaves no trace.
When all is finished, the people say,
"We did it ourselves."

I act virtuously.

I do not need rules

to be kind and just.

18th Verse

When the greatness of the Tao is present,
action arises from one's own heart.
When the greatness of the Tao is absent,
action comes from the rules
of "kindness and justice."

If you need rules to be kind and just,
if you <u>act</u> virtuous,
this is a sure sign that virtue is absent.
Thus we see the great hypocrisy.

When kinship falls into discord,
piety and rites of devotion arise.
When the country falls into chaos,
official loyalists will appear;
patriotism is born.

I am moral, profitable,

and a genius extraordinaire,

regardless of what any

transcript or bank

statement might say.

19th Verse

Give up sainthood, renounce wisdom,
and it will be a hundred times better for everyone.
Throw away morality and justice
and people will do the right thing.
Throw away industry and profit
and there will be no thieves.

All of these are outward forms alone;
they are not sufficient in themselves.

It is more important
to see the simplicity,
to realize one's true nature,
to cast off selfishness
and temper desire.

I am doing nothing.

Rather, I am being done.

20th Verse

Give up learning and you will be free
from all your cares.
What is the difference between yes and no?
What is the difference between good and evil?

Must I fear what others fear?
Should I fear desolation
when there is abundance?
Should I fear darkness
when that light is shining everywhere?

In spring, some go to the park and climb the terrace,
but I alone am drifting, not knowing where I am.
Like a newborn babe before it learns to smile,
I am alone, without a place to go.

Most people have too much;
I alone seem to be missing something.
Mine is indeed the mind of an ignoramus
in its unadulterated simplicity.
I am but a guest in this world.
While others rush about to get things done,
I accept what is offered.
I alone seem foolish,
earning little, spending less.

Other people strive for fame;
I avoid the limelight,
preferring to be left alone.
Indeed, I seem like an idiot:
no mind, no worries.

I drift like a wave on the ocean.
I blow as aimless as the wind.

All men settle down in their grooves;
I alone am stubborn and remain outside.
But wherein I am most different from others is
in knowing to take sustenance from the great Mother!

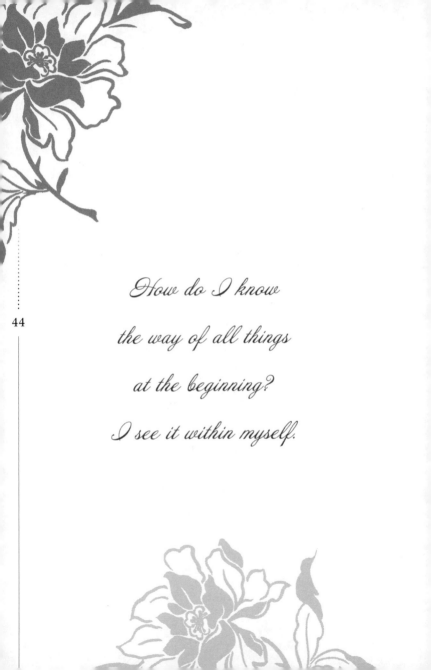

How do I know

the way of all things

at the beginning?

I see it within myself.

21st Verse

The greatest virtue is to follow the Tao
and the Tao alone.

The Tao is elusive and intangible.
Although formless and intangible,
it gives rise to form.
Although vague and elusive,
it gives rise to shapes.
Although dark and obscure,
it is the spirit, the essence,
the life breath of all things.

Throughout the ages, its name has been preserved
in order to recall the beginning of all things.
How do I know the ways of all things at the beginning?
I look inside myself and see what is within me.

46

I resist any

brokenness by being

flexible and bending

when storms appear.

22nd Verse

The flexible are preserved unbroken.
The bent become straight.
The empty are filled.
The exhausted become renewed.
The poor are enriched.
The rich are confounded.

Therefore the sage embraces the one.
Because he does not display himself,
people can see his light.
Because he has nothing to prove,
people can trust his words.
Because he does not know who he is,
people recognize themselves in him.
Because he has no goal in mind,
everything he does succeeds.

The old saying that the flexible are preserved
unbroken is surely right!
If you have truly attained wholeness,
everything will flock to you.

48

In all of nature,

no storm can last forever.

23rd Verse

To talk little is natural:
Fierce winds do not blow all morning;
a downpour of rain does not last the day.
Who does this? Heaven and earth.

But these are exaggerated, forced effects,
and that is why they cannot be sustained.
If heaven and earth cannot sustain a forced action,
how much less is man able to do?

Those who follow the Way
become one with the Way.
Those who follow goodness
become one with goodness.
Those who stray from the Way and goodness
become one with failure.

If you conform to the Way,
its power flows through you.
Your actions become those of nature,
your ways those of heaven.

Open yourself to the Tao
and trust your natural responses . . .
then everything will fall into place.

Boasting and showing

off are examples

of superfluous excesses.

These practices

must be uprooted,

thrown out,

and left behind forever.

24th Verse

If you stand on tiptoe, you cannot stand firmly.
If you take long steps, you cannot walk far.

Showing off does not reveal enlightenment.
Boasting will not produce accomplishment.
He who is self-righteous is not respected.
He who brags will not endure.

All these ways of acting are odious, distasteful.
They are superfluous excesses.
They are like a pain in the stomach,
a tumor in the body.

When walking the path of the Tao,
this is the very stuff that must be
uprooted, thrown out, and left behind.

I come from greatness.

I attract greatness.

I am greatness.

25th Verse

There was something formless and perfect
before the universe was born.
It is serene. Empty.
Solitary. Unchanging.
Infinite. Eternally present.
It is the Mother of the universe.
For lack of a better name,
I call it the Tao.

I call it great.
Great is boundless;
boundless is eternally flowing;
ever flowing, it is constantly returning.

Therefore, the Way is great,
heaven is great,
earth is great,
people are great.

Thus, to know humanity,
understand earth.
To know earth,
understand heaven.
To know heaven,
understand the Way.
To know the Way,
understand the great within yourself.

I have the ability

to stay poised and centered

regardless of what

goes before me.

26th Verse

The heavy is the root of the light.
The still is the master of unrest.

Realizing this,
the successful person is
poised and centered
in the midst of all activities;
although surrounded by opulence,
he is not swayed.

Why should the lord of the country
flit about like a fool?
If you let yourself be blown to and fro,
you lose touch with your root.
To be restless is to lose one's self-mastery.

What is a good man

but a bad man's teacher?

What is a bad man

but a good man's job?

27th Verse

A knower of the truth
travels without leaving a trace,
speaks without causing harm,
gives without keeping an account.
The door he shuts, though having no lock,
cannot be opened.
The knot he ties, though using no cord,
cannot be undone.

Be wise and help all beings impartially,
abandoning none.
Waste no opportunities.
This is called following the light.

What is a good man but a bad man's teacher?
What is a bad man but a good man's job?
If the teacher is not respected
and the student not cared for,
confusion will arise, however clever one is.
This is the great secret.

As I preserve

my original qualities,

I can do or govern anything.

I live with radical humility.

28th Verse

Know the strength of man,
but keep a woman's care!
Be a valley under heaven;
if you do, the constant virtue
will not fade away.
One will become like a child again.

Know the white,
keep to the black,
and be the pattern of the world.
To be the pattern of the world is
to move constantly in the path of virtue
without erring a single step,
and to return again to the infinite.

One who understands splendor
while holding to humility
acts in accord with eternal power.
To be the fountain of the world is
to live the abundant life of virtue.

When the unformed is formed into objects,
its original qualities are lost.
If you preserve your original qualities,
you can govern anything.
Truly, the best governor governs least.

There is a time for being ahead.

There is a time for being behind.

There is a time for being in motion.

There is a time for being at rest.

There is a time for being vigorous.

There is a time for being exhausted.

29th Verse

*Do you think you can take over the universe
and improve it?
I do not believe it can be done.*

*Everything under heaven is a sacred vessel
and cannot be controlled.
Trying to control leads to ruin.
Trying to grasp, we lose.*

*Allow your life to unfold naturally.
Know that it too is a vessel of perfection.
Just as you breathe in and breathe out,
there is a time for being ahead
and a time for being behind;
a time for being in motion
and a time for being at rest;
a time for being vigorous
and a time for being exhausted;
a time for being safe
and a time for being in danger.*

*To the sage
all of life is a movement toward perfection,
so what need has he
for the excessive, the extravagant, or the extreme?*

Whatever strains

with force will soon decay.

I eschew any and all forms

of violence. I take the line

of least resistance

in all of my actions.

30th Verse

One who would guide a leader of men in the uses of life
will warn him against the use of arms for conquest.
Weapons often turn upon the wielder.

Where armies settle,
nature offers nothing but briars and thorns.
After a great battle has been fought,
the land is cursed, the crops fail,
the earth lies stripped of its Motherhood.

After you have attained your purpose,
you must not parade your success,
you must not boast of your ability,
you must not feel proud;
you must rather regret that you had not been
able to prevent the war.

You must never think of conquering others by force.
Whatever strains with force
will soon decay.
It is not attuned to the Way.
Not being attuned to the Way,
its end comes all too soon.

64

I allow my highest nature

to come forward by bringing

love to the places where

I used to live in hatred.

31st Verse

Weapons are the tools of violence;
all decent men detest them.
Therefore, followers of the Tao never use them.

Arms serve evil.
They are the tools of those who oppose wise rule.
Use them only as a last resort.
For peace and quiet are dearest to the
decent man's heart,
and to him even a victory is no cause for rejoicing.

He who thinks triumph beautiful
is one with a will to kill,
and one with a will to kill
shall never prevail upon the world.

It is a good sign when man's higher nature
comes forward.
A bad sign when his lower nature comes forward.

With the slaughter of multitudes,
we have grief and sorrow.
Every victory is a funeral;
when you win a war,
you celebrate by mourning.

I trust in the perfect goodness

of the Tao to guide and

direct me wherever it will.

I allow my thoughts and

ideas to be carried by the

great wave of the Tao.

32nd Verse

The eternal Tao has no name.
Although simple and subtle,
no one in the world can master it.

If kings and lords could harness them,
the 10,000 things would naturally obey.
Heaven and earth would rejoice
with the dripping of sweet dew.
Everyone would live in harmony,
not by official decree,
but by their own goodness.

Once the whole is divided, the parts need names.
There are already enough names;
know when to stop.
Know when reason sets limits
to avoid peril.

Rivers and streams are born of the ocean,
and all creation is born of the Tao.
Just as all water flows back to become the ocean,
all creation flows back to become the Tao.

I am replacing my desire for power

over others with my efforts

to understand and master myself

in any and all situations.

The things I love . . .

I have to learn to leave alone.

33rd Verse

One who understands others has knowledge;
one who understands himself has wisdom.
Mastering others requires force;
mastering the self needs strength.

If you realize that you have enough,
you are truly rich.

One who gives himself to his position
surely lives long.
One who gives himself to the Tao
surely lives forever.

70

By not <u>claiming</u> greatness,

I <u>achieve</u> greatness.

34th Verse

*The Great Way is universal;
it can apply to the left or the right.
All beings depend on it for life;
even so, it does not take possession of them.*

*It accomplishes its purpose,
but makes no claim for itself.
It covers all creatures like the sky,
but does not dominate them.*

*All things return to it as to their home,
but it does not lord it over them;
thus, it may be called "great."*

*The sage imitates this conduct:
By not claiming greatness,
the sage achieves greatness.*

When I look for it,

there is nothing to see.

When I listen for it,

there is nothing to hear.

When I use it,

it cannot be exhausted.

This is the great Tao.

35th Verse

All men will come to him
who keeps to the one.
They flock to him and receive no harm,
for in him they find peace, security, and happiness.

Music and dining are passing pleasures,
yet they cause people to stop.
How bland and insipid are the things of this world
when one compares them to the Tao!

When you look for it, there is nothing to see.
When you listen for it, there is nothing to hear.
When you use it, it cannot be exhausted.

74

I seek out obscurity

by suppressing any desires for

attention or recognition.

36th Verse

Should you want to contain something,
you must deliberately let it expand.
Should you want to weaken something,
you must deliberately let it grow strong.
Should you want to eliminate something,
you must deliberately allow it to flourish.
Should you want to take something away,
you must deliberately grant it access.

The lesson here is called
the wisdom of obscurity.
The gentle outlasts the strong.
The obscure outlasts the obvious.

Fish cannot leave deep waters,
and a country's weapons should not be displayed.

76

The Tao does nothing . . .

but leaves nothing undone.

37th Verse

The Tao does nothing,
but leaves nothing undone.

If powerful men
could center themselves in it,
the whole world would be transformed
by itself, in its natural rhythms.

When life is simple,
pretenses fall away;
our essential natures shine through.

By not wanting, there is calm,
and the world will straighten itself.
When there is silence,
one finds the anchor of the universe within oneself.

I trust my essential nature.

I let go of all polarities,

and I live in the indivisible

oneness of the Tao. Goodness

and Godness are one, and

I trust who I am,

a child of God.

38th Verse

A truly good man is not aware of his goodness
and is therefore good.
A foolish man tries to be good
and is therefore not good.

The master does nothing,
yet he leaves nothing undone.
The ordinary man is always doing things,
yet many more are left to be done.

The highest virtue is to act without a sense of self.
The highest kindness is to give without condition.
The highest justice is to see without preference.

When the Tao is lost, there is goodness.
When goodness is lost, there is morality.
When morality is lost, there is ritual.
Ritual is the husk of true faith,
the beginning of chaos.

The great master follows his own nature
and not the trappings of life.
It is said:
"He stays with the fruit and not the fluff."
"He stays with the firm and not the flimsy."
"He stays with the true and not the false."

I am a piece of the whole,

and I act in accordance with

the wholeness of the Tao.

39th Verse

These things from ancient times arise from one:
The sky is whole and clear.
The earth is whole and firm.
The spirit is whole and full.
The 10,000 things are whole, and the country is upright.
All these are in virtue of wholeness.

When man interferes with the Tao,
the sky becomes filthy,
the earth becomes depleted,
the equilibrium crumbles,
creatures become extinct.

Therefore, nobility is rooted in humility;
loftiness is based on lowliness.
This is why noble people refer to themselves
as alone, lacking, and unworthy.

The pieces of a chariot are useless
unless they work in accordance with the whole.
A man's life brings nothing
unless he lives in accordance with the whole universe.
Playing one's part
in accordance with the universe
is true humility.

Truly, too much honor means no honor.
It is not wise to shine like jade and
resound like stone chimes.

I bow to the

All-Creating Power

from which I came and

to which I am returning.

40th Verse

Returning is the motion of the Tao.
Yielding is the way of the Tao.
The 10,000 things are born of being.
Being is born of nonbeing.

By following the Way,

I do not become complicated,

extraordinary, or prominent.

Rather, I become subtle,

simple, and uncomplicated.

41st Verse

A great scholar hears of the Tao
and begins diligent practice.
A middling scholar hears of the Tao
and retains some and loses some.
An inferior scholar hears of the Tao
and roars with ridicule.
Without that laugh, it would not be the Tao.

So there are constructive sayings on this:
The way of illumination seems dark,
going forward seems like retreat,
the easy way seems hard,
true power seems weak,
true purity seems tarnished,
true clarity seems obscure,
the greatest art seems unsophisticated,
the greatest love seems indifferent,
the greatest wisdom seems childish.

The Tao is hidden and nameless;
the Tao alone nourishes and brings
everything to fulfillment.

I release attachment

to all objects, status,

people, and institutions.

I gain by losing.

I lose by gaining.

42nd Verse

The Tao gave birth to one.
One gave birth to two.
Two gave birth to three.
And three begat the 10,000 things.
The 10,000 things carry yin and embrace yang;
they achieve harmony by combining these forces.

People suffer at the thought of being
without parents, without food, or without worth.
Yet this is the very way that
kings and lords once described themselves.
For one gains by losing,
and loses by gaining.

What others taught, I teach.
The violent do not die a natural death.
That is my fundamental teaching.

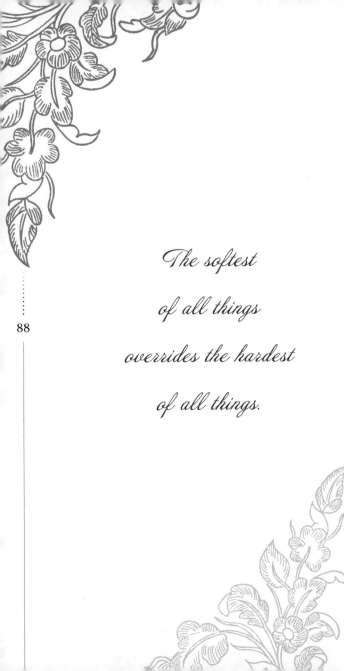

The softest

of all things

overrides the hardest

of all things.

43rd Verse

The softest of all things
overrides the hardest of all things.
That without substance enters where there is no space.
Hence I know the value of nonaction.

Teaching without words,
performing without actions—
few in the world can grasp it—
that is the master's way.
Rare indeed are those
who obtain the bounty of this world.

I let go

of my need for more,

and live in a state

of pure gratitude.

Giving is replacing

my demand for more.

44th Verse

Which means more to you,
you or your renown?
Which brings more to you,
you or what you own?
I say what you gain
is more trouble than what you lose.

Love is the fruit of sacrifice.
Wealth is the fruit of generosity.

A contented man is never disappointed.
He who knows when to stop is preserved from peril,
only thus can you endure long.

92

The experience

of inner peace

is my true gauge

of all accomplishments.

45th Verse

The greatest perfection seems imperfect,
and yet its use is inexhaustible.
The greatest fullness seems empty,
and yet its use is endless.

Great straightness seems twisted.
Great intelligence seems stupid.
Great eloquence seems awkward.
Great truth seems false.
Great discussion seems silent.

Activity conquers cold;
inactivity conquers heat.
Stillness and tranquility set things in order
in the universe.

94

There is no greater loss than

losing my connection to the Tao.

I find the bliss of eternity

in my contentment.

46th Verse

When the world has the Way,
running horses are retired to till the fields.
When the world lacks the Way,
warhorses are bred in the countryside.

There is no greater loss than losing the Tao,
no greater curse than covetousness,
no greater tragedy than discontentment;
the worst of faults is wanting more—always.

Contentment alone is enough.
Indeed, the bliss of eternity
can be found in your contentment.

Without going out the door,

I can know the world.

Without looking out the window,

I can see the ways of heaven.

47th Verse

Without going out the door,
know the world.
Without looking out the window,
you may see the ways of heaven.

The farther one goes,
the less one knows.

Therefore the sage does not venture forth
and yet knows,
does not look
and yet names,
does not strive
and yet attains completion.

In order to enliven

my experience of the Tao

and live by its principles,

I practice decreasing

my reliance on things.

48th Verse

Learning consists of daily accumulating.
The practice of the Tao consists of daily diminishing;
decreasing and decreasing, until doing nothing.
When nothing is done, nothing is left undone.

99

True mastery can be gained
by letting things go their own way.
It cannot be gained by interfering.

It is my choice to be kind to those

who are kind. It is my choice

to be kind to those who are unkind,

because the nature of my being

is kindness, and that is all

I have to give away.

49th Verse

The sage has no fixed mind;
he is aware of the needs of others.

Those who are good he treats with goodness.
Those who are bad he also treats with goodness
because the nature of his being is good.

He is kind to the kind.
He is also kind to the unkind
because the nature of his being is kindness.

He is faithful to the faithful;
he is also faithful to the unfaithful.
The sage lives in harmony with all below heaven.
He sees everything as his own self;
he loves everyone as his own child.

All people are drawn to him.
He behaves like a little child.

I am an

immortal spiritual being

having a temporary

human experience.

50th Verse

Between birth and death,
three in ten are followers of life;
three in ten are followers of death.
And men just passing from birth to death
also number three in ten.

Why is this so?
Because they clutch to life
and cling to this passing world.

But there is one out of ten, they say, so sure of life
that tigers and wild bulls keep clear.
Weapons turn from him on the battlefield,
rhinoceroses have no place to horn him,
tigers find no place for claws,
and soldiers have no place to thrust their blades.

Why is this so?
Because he dwells in that place
where death cannot enter.

Realize your essence
and you will witness the end without ending.

The Great Tao

has no expectations for me,

no demands, no battles

or wars to fight,

and no history

to live up to.

51st Verse

The Way connects all living beings to their Source.
It springs into existence,
unconscious, perfect, free;
takes on a physical body;
lets circumstances complete it.

Therefore all beings honor the Way
and value its virtue.
They have not been commanded to worship the Tao
and do homage to virtue,
but they always do so spontaneously.

The Tao gives them life.
Virtue nourishes and nurtures them,
rears and shelters and protects them.
The Tao produces but does not possess;
the Tao gives without expecting;
the Tao fosters growth without ruling.
This is called hidden virtue.

All under heaven

have a common beginning.

This beginning is the

mother of the world

and my eternal mother.

52nd Verse

All under heaven have a common beginning.
This beginning is the Mother of the world.
Having known the Mother,
we may proceed to know her children.
Having known the children,
we should go back and hold on to the Mother.

Keep your mouth shut,
guard the senses,
and life is ever full.
Open your mouth,
always be busy,
and life is beyond hope.

Seeing the small is called clarity;
keeping flexible is called strength.
Using the shining radiance,
you return again to the light
and save yourself misfortune.

This is called
the practice of eternal light.

If I have even a little sense,

I walk in the Great Way,

and my only fear is straying.

I live honorably.

I see myself in all others.

53rd Verse

If I have even just a little sense,
I should walk in the Great Way,
and my only fear would be straying.

The Great Way is very smooth and straight,
and yet the people prefer devious paths.
That is why the court is corrupt,
the fields lie in waste,
the granaries are empty.

Dressing magnificently,
wearing a sharp sword,
stuffing oneself with food and drink,
amassing wealth to the extent of not knowing
what to do with it,
is being like a robber.

I say this pomp at the expense of others
is like the boasting of thieves after a looting.
This is not the Tao.

I am like

a great wave of energy

that illuminates a room.

Everyone sees the light

and becomes affected.

54th Verse

Whoever is planted in the Tao
will not be rooted up.
Whoever embraces the Tao
will not slip away.

Generations honor generations endlessly.
Cultivated in the self, virtue is realized;
cultivated in the family, virtue overflows;
cultivated in the community, virtue increases;
cultivated in the state, virtue abounds.

The Tao is everywhere;
it has become everything.
To truly see it, see it as it is.
In a person, see it as a person;
in a family, see it as a family;
in a country, see it as a country;
in the world, see it as the world.

How do I know this is true?
By looking inside myself.

I attract the cooperative

power of the Tao when

I release the need to control

anyone's life, including my own.

55th Verse

He who is in harmony with the Tao
is like a newborn child.
Deadly insects will not sting him.
Wild beasts will not attack him.
Birds of prey will not strike him.
Bones are weak, muscles are soft,
yet his grasp is firm.

He has not experienced the union of man and woman,
but is whole.
His manhood is strong.
He screams all day without becoming hoarse.
This is perfect harmony.

To know harmony is to know the changeless;
to know the changeless is to have insight.
Things in harmony with the Tao remain;
things that are forced grow for a while,
but then wither away.
This is not the Tao.
And whatever is against the Tao soon ceases to be.

Those who know do not talk.

Those who talk do not know.

The less I care about

the approval of others,

the more approval

I receive.

56th Verse

Those who know do not talk.
Those who talk do not know.

Block all the passages!
Close your mouth,
cordon off your senses,
blunt your sharpness,
untie your knots,
soften your glare,
settle your dust.
This is primal union or the secret embrace.

One who knows this secret
is not moved by attachment or aversion,
swayed by profit or loss,
nor touched by honor or disgrace.
He is far beyond the cares of men
yet comes to hold the dearest place in their hearts.

This, therefore, is the highest state of man.

I work at allowing all others

to trust in their highest nature

rather than imposing my rules and

regulations on them. Moreover,

I am free to be myself.

I do not have to live

by anyone else's rules.

57th Verse

If you want to be a great leader,
you must learn to follow the Tao.
Stop trying to control.
Let go of fixed plans and concepts,
and the world will govern itself.

How do I know this is so?
Because in this world,
the greater the restrictions and prohibitions,
the more people are impoverished;
the more advanced the weapons of state,
the darker the nation;
the more artful and crafty the plan,
the stranger the outcome;
the more laws are posted,
the more thieves appear.

Therefore the sage says:
I take no action and people are reformed.
I enjoy peace and people become honest.
I do nothing and people become rich.
If I keep from imposing on people,
they become themselves.

Bad fortune

has good fortune

hiding within it,

and good fortune

is what bad fortune

hides in.

58th Verse

When the ruler knows his own heart,
the people are simple and pure.
When he meddles with their lives,
they become restless and disturbed.

Bad fortune is what good fortune leans on;
good fortune is what bad fortune hides in.
Who knows the ultimate end of this process?
Is there no norm of right?
Yet what is normal soon becomes abnormal;
peoples's confusion is indeed long-standing.

Thus the master is content to serve as an example
and not to impose his will.
He is pointed but does not pierce;
he straightens but does not disrupt;
he illuminates but does not dazzle.

I practice living

without limits by

gathering virtue

and modeling it.

59th Verse

In governing people and serving nature,
nothing surpasses thrift and moderation.

Restraint begins with giving up one's own ideas.
This depends on virtue gathered in the past.
If there is a good store of virtue,
then nothing is impossible.
If nothing is impossible, then there are no limits.
If a man knows no limits, he is fit to lead.

This is the way to be deeply rooted and
firmly planted in the Tao,
the secret of long life and lasting vision.

When I refrain

from thoughts of harm

directed toward others,

I accumulate all

the benefits of life.

60th Verse

Governing a large county
is like frying a small fish.
You spoil it with too much poking.

Approach the universe with the Tao
and evil will have no power.
Not that evil is not powerful,
but its power will not be used to harm others.
Not only will it not do harm to others,
but the sage himself will also be protected.

If only the ruler and his people would
refrain from harming each other,
all the benefits of life would accumulate
in the kingdom.

My loved
ones and I cannot
and will not be impacted
by the presence of evil anywhere
in the world. By staying calm
and under the radar,
others will ultimately
join me in friendship and trust.

61st Verse

*A great country is like the lowland,
toward which all streams flow.
It is the reservoir of all under heaven,
the feminine of the world.
The female overcomes the male with stillness,
by lowering herself through her quietness.*

*So if a great country lowers itself before a small one,
it wins friendship and trust.
And if a small country can lower itself before a great one,
it will win over that "great" country.
The one wins by stooping;
the other, by remaining low.*

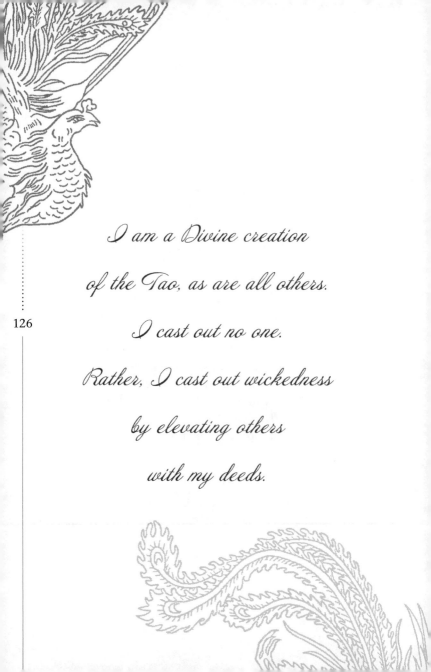

I am a Divine creation

of the Tao, as are all others.

I cast out no one.

Rather, I cast out wickedness

by elevating others

with my deeds.

62nd Verse

The Tao is the treasure-house,
the true nature,
the secret Source of everything.
It is the treasure of the good man
and the refuge of the bad.

If a person seems wicked,
do not cast him away.
Awaken him with your words,
elevate him with your deeds,
repay his injury with your kindness.
Do not cast him away;
cast away his wickedness.

Thus when a new leader is chosen,
do not offer to help him
with your wealth or your expertise.
Help him to meditate on the principle;
offer instead to teach him about the Tao.

Why did the ancients make so much of the principle?
Is it not because it is the Source of all good,
and the remedy for all evil?
It is the most noble thing in the world.

I see simplicity

in the complicated.

I do great things

while they are small.

I can get anywhere

from here.

63rd Verse

Practice nonaction.
Work without doing.
Taste the tasteless.
Magnify the small, increase the few.
Reward bitterness with care.
See simplicity in the complicated.
Achieve greatness in little things.

Take on difficulties while they are still easy;
do great things while they are still small.
The sage does not attempt anything very big,
and thus achieves greatness.

If you agree too easily, you will be little trusted;
because the sage always confronts difficulties,
he never experiences them.

A journey of

a thousand miles

begins with one step.

A tree grows from one seedling.

A tower starts with one brick.

64th Verse

What is at rest is easily managed.
What is not yet manifest is easy to prevent.
The brittle is easily shattered;
the small is easily scattered.

Act before things exist;
manage them before there is disorder.
Remember:
A tree that fills a man's embrace grows from a seedling.
A tower nine stories high starts with one brick.
A journey of a thousand miles begins with a single step.

Act and destroy it;
grasp it and lose it.
The sage does not act, and so is not defeated.
He does not grasp and therefore does not lose.
People usually fail when they are on the verge of success.
So give as much care at the end as at the beginning,
then there will be no failure.

The sage does not treasure what is difficult to attain.
He does not collect precious things;
he learns not to hold on to ideas.
He helps the 10,000 things find their own nature
but does not venture to lead them by the nose.

Because I know that

I do not know,

I am guided

to find my own way.

65th Verse

*The ancient ones were simple-hearted
and blended with the common people.
They did not shine forth;
they did not rule with cleverness,
so the nation was blessed.*

*When they think that they know the answers,
people are difficult to guide.
When they know they do not know,
people can find their own way.*

*Not using cunning to govern a country
is good fortune for the country.
The simplest pattern is the clearest.
Content with an ordinary life,
you can show all people the way
back to their own true nature.*

134

I do not put myself

above others or see myself

as superior to anyone.

I am like the great ocean,

where all streams flow to me

because I stay low, and thus,

I am a servant to all.

66th Verse

Why is the sea king of a hundred streams?
Because it lies below them.
Humility gives it its power.

Therefore, those desiring a position
above others must speak humbly.
Those desiring to lead must follow.

Thus it is that when a sage stands above the people,
they do not feel the heaviness of his weight;
and when he stands in front of the people,
they do not feel hurt.

The sage stays low
so the world never tires of exalting him.
He remains a servant
so the world never tires of making him its king.

I live the

three treasures of mercy,

frugality, and humility

in all of my dealings

with others.

67th Verse

All the world talks about my Tao
with such familiarity—
what folly!
The Tao is not something found at the marketplace
or passed on from father to son.
It is not something gained by knowing
or lost by forgetting.
If the Tao were like this,
it would have been lost and forgotten long ago.

I have three treasures, which I hold fast
and watch closely.
The first is mercy.
The second is frugality.
The third is humility.

From mercy comes courage.
From frugality comes generosity.
From humility comes leadership.
Now if one were bold but had no mercy,
if one were broad but were not frugal,
if one went ahead without humility,
one would die.

Love vanquishes all attackers,
it is impregnable in defense.
When heaven wants to protect someone,
does it send an army?
No, it protects him with love.

Whatever I fight

weakens me.

What I cooperate with

strengthens me.

68th Verse

A good soldier is not violent.
A good fighter is not angry.
Good winners do not contend.
Good employers serve their workers.
The best leader follows the will of the people.

All of them embody the virtue of noncompetition.
This is called the virtue of noncontending.
This is called employing the powers of others.

This since ancient times has been known
as the ultimate unity with heaven.

There is no greater

misfortune than feeling

I have an enemy,

for when I have an enemy,

there is no room for God.

69th Verse

There is a saying among soldiers:
I dare not make the first move
but would rather play the guest;
I dare not advance an inch
but would rather withdraw a foot.

This is called
going forward without advancing,
pushing back without using weapons.

There is no greater misfortune
than feeling "I have an enemy";
for when "I" and "enemy" exist together,
there is no room left for my treasure.

Thus, when two opponents meet,
the one without an enemy
will surely triumph.

When armies are evenly matched,
the one with compassion wins.

I want to think like

God thinks, to act as God acts,

to live a God-realized life.

70th Verse

*My teachings are very easy to understand
and very easy to practice;
yet so few in this world understand,
and so few are able to practice.*

*My words have an ancestor;
my deeds have a lord.
The people have no knowledge of this,
therefore they have no knowledge of me.*

*This is why the sage dresses plainly,
even though his interior is filled
with precious gems.*

144

I trust that a happy,

contented mind

that is sick of being sick

will have a happy,

contented body.

71st Verse

Knowing ignorance is strength.
Ignoring knowledge is sickness.

Only when we are sick of our sickness
shall we cease to be sick.
The sage is not sick but is sick of sickness;
this is the secret of health.

My body is perfect,

born at precisely the right time,

and this is my perfect age.

I accept myself as I am,

and I surrender

to the natural course

of my body's destiny.

72nd Verse

When people lack a sense of awe,
there will be disaster.
When people do not fear worldly power,
a greater power will arrive.

Do not limit the view of yourself.
Do not despise the conditions of your birth.
Do not resist the natural course of your life.
In this way you will never weary of this world.

Therefore, the sage knows himself
but makes no show of himself;
loves himself
but does not exalt himself.
He prefers what is within to what is without.

It is my intention

to emulate heaven's way

by listening more, speaking less,

and trusting that my answers

will come without any screaming.

I slow my pace so that it harmonizes

with heaven's way.

73rd Verse

Bold action against others leads to death.
Bold action in harmony with the Tao leads to life.
Both of these things
sometimes benefit
and sometimes injure.

It is heaven's way to conquer without striving.
It does not speak, yet it is answered.
It does not ask, yet it is supplied with all that it needs.
It does not hurry, yet it completes everything on time.

The net of heaven catches all;
its mesh is coarse,
but nothing slips through.

I realize that all things change;

therefore, there is nothing

for me to hold on to.

By not fearing death,

there is nothing

that I cannot achieve.

74th Verse

If you realize that all things change,
there is nothing you will try to hold on to.
If you are not afraid of dying,
there is nothing you cannot achieve.

There is always a lord of death.
He who takes the place of the lord of death
is like one who cuts with the blade
of a master carpenter.
Whoever cuts with the blade of a master carpenter
is sure to cut his own hands.

I place fewer and fewer

demands upon others,

and especially myself.

I am free to commune

with nature, work, play, read,

or just do nothing.

75th Verse

When taxes are too high,
people go hungry.
When the government is too intrusive,
people lose their spirit.

Act for the people's benefit;
trust them, leave them alone.

I choose to be strong

by being soft and pliable

rather than inflexible,

brittle, and hard.

76th Verse

A man is born gentle and weak;
at his death he is hard and stiff.
All things, including the grass and trees,
are soft and pliable in life;
dry and brittle in death.

Stiffness is thus a companion of death;
flexibility a companion of life.
An army that cannot yield
will be defeated.
A tree that cannot bend
will crack in the wind.

The hard and stiff will be broken;
the soft and supple will prevail.

I can keep on giving

because there is no end

to my wealth.

I am pleased to offer

my surpluses

to others.

77th Verse

The way of heaven
is like drawing a bow:
The high is lowered,
the low is raised.

When it is surplus, it reduces;
when it is deficient, it increases.
The Tao of mankind is the opposite:
It reduces the deficiency in order to add to the surplus.
It strips the needy to serve those who have too much.

Only the one who has the Tao offers
his surplus to others.
What man has more than enough
and gives it to the world?
Only the man of the Tao.

The master can keep giving
because there is no end to his wealth.
He acts without expectation,
succeeds without taking credit,
and does not think that he is better
than anyone else.

I remain serene

in the midst

of sorrow

and therefore

prevent evil

from entering

my heart.

78th Verse

*Nothing in the world is softer
and weaker than water.
But for attacking the hard, the unyielding,
nothing can surpass it.
There is nothing like it.*

*The weak overcomes the strong;
the soft surpasses the hard.
In all the world, there is no one who does not know this,
but no one can master the practice.*

*Therefore the master remains
serene in the midst of sorrow;
evil cannot enter his heart.
Because he has given up helping,
he is people's greatest help.*

True words appear paradoxical.

Someone must risk

returning injury with kindness,

or hostility will never turn

to goodwill. I choose

to preclude any future

conflict by emanating

love and kindness.

79th Verse

After a bitter quarrel, some resentment remains.
What can one do about it?
Being content with what you have
is always best in the end.

Someone must risk returning injury with kindness,
or hostility will never turn to goodwill.
So the wise always give without expecting gratitude.

One with true virtue
always seeks a way to give.
One who lacks true virtue
always seeks a way to get.
To the giver comes the fullness of life;
to the taker, just an empty hand.

I live in a state

of radical appreciation.

I give humble thanks

for all that I have.

Paradise is

wherever I am.

80th Verse

Imagine a small country with few people.
They have weapons and do not employ them;
they enjoy the labor of their hands
and do not waste time inventing laborsaving machines.

They take death seriously and do not travel far.
Since they dearly love their homes,
they are not interested in travel.
Although they have boats and carriages,
no one uses them.

163

They are content with healthy food,
pleased with useful clothing,
satisfied in snug homes,
and protective of their way of life.

Although they live within sight of their neighbors,
and crowing cocks and barking dogs can be
heard across the way,
they leave each other in peace
while they grow old and die.

164

I accumulate less, give more,

and release my attachment

to everything in the world

of the 10,000 things.

81st Verse

True words are not beautiful;
beautiful words are not true.
Good men do not argue;
those who argue are not good.
Those who have virtue do not look for faults;
those who look for faults have no virtue.

Sages do not accumulate anything
but give everything to others;
having more, the more they give.

Heaven does good to all,
doing no evil to anyone.
The sage imitates it, acting
for the good of all,
and opposing himself to no one.

Acknowledgments

I thank the translators and authors
of the following ten books:

*The Essential Tao: An Initiation into the Heart of Taoism
through the Authentic <u>Tao Te Ching</u> and the Inner Teachings of
<u>Chuang Tzu,</u> translated and presented by Thomas Cleary*

*The Illustrated Tao Te Ching:
A New Translation with Commentary,* by Stephen Hodge

Tao Te Ching, by Lao Tsu;
translated by Gia-Fu Feng and Jane English

Tao Te Ching: The Definitive Edition, by Lao Tzu;
translation and commentary by Jonathan Star

Tao Te Ching: A New English Version,
by Stephen Mitchell

Tao-Te-Ching: A New Translation, by Lao-Tzu;
translated by Derek Bryce and Léon Wieger

Tao Te Ching: A New Translation, by Lao Tzu;
translated by Sam Hamill

Tao Te Ching, by Lao Tzu; translated by John C. H. Wu

A Warrior Blends with Life: A Modern Tao,
by Michael LaTorra

The Way of Life According to Lao Tzu,
translated by Witter Bynner

About the Author

Wayne W. Dyer, Ph.D., is an internationally renowned author and speaker in the field of self-development. He's the author of more than 30 books, has created many audio programs and videos, and has appeared on thousands of television and radio shows. His books *Manifest Your Destiny, Wisdom of the Ages, There's a Spiritual Solution to Every Problem,* and *The New York Times* bestsellers *10 Secrets for Success and Inner Peace, The Power of Intention, Inspiration,* and *Change Your Thoughts—Change Your Life* have all been featured as National Public Television specials.

Wayne holds a doctorate in educational counseling from Wayne State University and was an associate professor at St. John's University in New York.

Website: **www.DrWayneDyer.com**

Notes

Notes

Notes

Notes

Notes

Notes

Notes

Notes

Notes

Notes

Notes